Freed

Freed

Book of Poems

Nicole Telfer

Rev. date: 04/24/2018

To order additional copies of this book, contact:
Xlibris
1-888-795-4274
www.Xlibris.com
Orders@Xlibris.com
764373

To Nicolette
We survived, sis. I love you.

To my aunt Charlyne
Thank you for instilling this idea in me, and thank you for encouraging me to pursue my passions and dreams. Most importantly, thank you for being part of the village that raised me.

CONTENTS

1

Overcome

To get the better of in a struggle or conflict;
conquer; defeat; to overcome the enemy

Therefore, I win.

DEAD INSIDE

When I was younger, I used to always convince God that I'd make a
perfect addition to his angels
This world didn't need me, and I didn't want to be here anyways
If being alive meant that I would always be a victim because I was a
girl and beautiful and Black, then I was willing to forfeit my existence
When I was younger, I used to hold my breath and close my eyes a lot
That's how I practiced absence
Especially when he placed himself on top of me
Don't know what it's like to feel like a dead little girl?
It's not being able to have friends over because they are just as scared
as you
It's not wanting to go home after school because fear warned you not to
It's everyone around you knowing that you're unhappy but says *she's just
a child, what does she know about feelings?*
It's being your sister's protector even though you needed protection too
Having to offer up your body to keep hers safe from the monster who
lived under your bed
And terrorized you when no one was looking, just like in the movies
you watched.

I still have a hard time saying *no* to pain,
But how do you say *no* when pain calls you friend?
When pain silences you? When pain is all you have ever known?

Or here's a better question:
Where was happiness when you begged for her to come and save you?

YOUR LETTER

I still couldn't feel sorry for you after reading it
You didn't feel sorry for me when you made my knees best friends with
the carpet in your room,
Or when you made your mouth familiar with parts of my body,
Or when you burned me with a hot skillet for not complying,
Or when you nearly choked me to death for spitting your urine out of
my mouth
What I'm trying to say is—
Everything that you are going through now is because you deserve it
You don't get to be happy because you took that away from me before
I could even understand what happiness felt like
You don't get to experience peace because you made me live in fear my
entire childhood
Because of you, I expect men to treat me like I am beneath them
I expect them to touch my body without my permission
Like you have done over and over again
I don't expect them to hold doors open for me or treat me like I am
valuable
Because of you, I don't want to commit to anyone
I don't think I am capable of being in love
Every time I find someone, I think that he will be just like you,
The sweetest one day, and a monster the next
I think that he will hurt me
Physically.

Mentally.
Because of you, I choose not to love.

So, thank you for your letter
That was really thoughtful of you,
But I think you have already done enough damage.

DAMN TRUTH

My entire life I have been taught that defending myself is too dangerous,
too risky
I have been taught that my body is not mine.
Anyone can borrow it for their pleasure,
Stay for the night and then leave the next day with everything broken
for me to put back together—
After all, it is a woman's job to clean up the messy house
She may live there, but she does not own it.

If she says she is being abused, please believe her.

RECLAIMING MY BODY

The only time you allowed me to speak was when you forced me to say
it's okay after you said *I'm sorry* over and over again
The only time you gave me assurance was when you said *this is the last
time I'm doing this, I promise*
Over and over again
That was all there was to you, repetition
Repetition in lying,
Repetition in hurting me,
Repetition in controlling me
Controlling my body.

But I have decided to take back what belongs to me
You have had ownership for far too long
I will not go according to societal norms that demand women to give
every part of them to those who ask
This time, I am reclaiming my body
I will spit life into her lungs and let her exhale all the pain she has felt
And though you have done much damage
I will put her back together
Limb by limb,
Bone by bone,
Because this body deserves love.

MAGICIAN

At the end of every day,
When he was through with making me less and less of a person,
He would place a glass of apple juice in my hands
He knew it was my favorite
He would tell me that he was done for the day
That I could go watch tv and relax
Until his teeth were horny for my blood again.

And voila,
He forgets.
And voila,
I somehow forget too.

RAPE CULTURE PRIVILEGE

Rest in peace to the bodies taken because of rape
Not only the physical bodies, but spiritual ones as well
When the enemy robbed you of your sacred temple and made it his home
Without permission and without warning
You probably thought that because God dwells within you, he would've kept it safe
And now you're struggling, trying to make your temple whole again
But the stains are not going away
The seed has already been planted and the damage has been done.

Rape culture privilege is society overlooking rape
Rape culture privilege is people asking *are you sure you said no?*
Is rapists believing that you enjoyed it
Is being forced to be present when your body is absent
When your body betrayed you but you still have to love her
Because everyone else does not.

Rape culture privilege is Brock Turner
Who was lucky enough to use his White privilege as well and was sentenced to a play room timeout
Three months to be exact.
Rape culture privilege is Bill Cosby
Who is still free to this day.

1 in 6 women are raped in their lifetime
That means my five closest girl friends and I,

The women in my family,
My unborn daughters.

Dear America, please do better,
Protect the beautiful beings that give life to this world.

CONSISTENCY

That night, I wrapped my fist in a warm cloth
As it throbbed from me punching the wall
I was angry
Angry at Mom, angry at those who knew, angry at the one who was watching,
God.
That night, I hid all of my head scarves hoping that he wouldn't bother with me
He did not like when my hair was in his face
It's itchy, tie it up
That night, I looked at myself in the mirror
Everything about me seemed unfamiliar
That night, my body was not in my control
Every night my body was not in my control
That night, like every other night, I hated myself
Too afraid to tell him *stop* or *no* or *how about you go find a girlfriend*
That night, Mom came home from work and told me don't forget to pray before bed
I read my Bible with bitterness,
With confusion because if Eve was created from Adam's rib, then why are men so heartless toward women?
Why can't I find protection in men?
Why am I so afraid of them?
Why was I so afraid of him?

He must have read the Bible every night too,
Had it stuffed between his sinful bed where my tank tops were located
Maybe that's why he felt more powerful than me,
He believed that he was already given permission.

MY ONLY WISH

I never wanted you to be added to the mass incarceration of Black men
I never wanted to tell anyone, not even the police
I never wanted to be taken away from our home
I only wanted you to stop.

UNWRITTEN LETTER

I prepared the envelope by placing the stamp precisely on the right-hand corner
The letter, on the other hand, is incomplete
What do you say to someone who is the cause of the mental damage that you are still trying to repair?

> *Hey you! How's everything? Can't wait for you to get home.*
> No.
> *Hey, I received your letter. Thanks for thinking of me.*
> No.

I can't seem to find a perfect way to write this letter
Because I still can't face you
I still can't look at myself in the mirror and smile
I still can't love myself the way that I am supposed to
How the hell am I supposed to bring you comfort when you have groomed me to be uncomfortable with myself?
You hated the way I walked, so I hated the way I walked
You hated my gap, so I got braces to close it
I didn't like my body because it attracted you and every other grown man.

I can't write this letter because I am still afraid to be honest with you
But at some point, I am going to have to face my past
If I want to learn to love, I'm going to have to confront those [you] who hurt me,
And so it begins:

Dear Monster,
I did get your letter and I hope you get mine. Just to be clear,
I have no intention of seeing you again. My life has been better since
you have been gone. This time, I choose peace. I choose me.

LITTLE ME

Every day I wish that I could have been there for the little me
I would sit in her room and wait for her to run in crying just so I could hold her
I would tell her that I believe her, and that this nightmare won't last forever
I would be everything that she wanted
A fairy to grant her every wish, even if she wished to run from home
I would be Superwoman, to defeat the villain and cast him away forever
I would be a friend, so she wouldn't have to ask herself *why me* all the time
I probably would not have been able to answer her question, but I would have been there so that we could ask God together
I am not sure why she had to go through this, nor am I sure about the lesson she was supposed to learn
But I do know that today she is stronger than she has ever been
I'm witnessing it for myself.

SHE STILL FEARS

I still feel your heavy hands wrapped around my arms,
Those same heavy hands when I tried to run away from you that night
I didn't want to please you, I was too tired.
I still feel your heavy hands
Every time another man touches me.

THE EVENING BEFORE
HIS BIRTHDAY

The phone began to ring.
You are receiving a call from the correctional facility. The caller is low on minutes. If you wish to accept this call, please press 3.

Hey hun, how is everything? It says you are low on minutes.
I will have to put more money into your account.

The evening before his birthday, she demanded that I speak to him
He's still your family and he's not a bad guy
There she goes again, filtering out all the pain that he caused me.
I grabbed the phone from her with all the anger I had in me

Hi, Nicole. Good hearing your voice.
I miss you and your sister. I'll be home soon,
I know you guys miss me too.

And there he goes again, assuming that I ever liked him
Believing that what he did was excusable.
I didn't tell him happy birthday, that would have been too nice of me
I didn't speak much, my heart wouldn't allow me
I wanted to tell him to stop asking for me
To stop asking for my sister
But instead,
I'll just play along
Like I did as a child,
As the victim,
And wait until he gets my letter.

I AM HERE

I am still alive
My battle was given to me for a reason
This means that my strength saved someone's life
It saved my life, too
Because I am still alive.

LIFETIME MOVIES

Every Sunday, Mom and I would watch Lifetime movies all day
We would eat ice cream in bed along with our dinner
Mom and I cuddled and talked through every single movie, yelling at
the senseless characters
On Sundays, I was a happy little girl.
Because on Sundays, Mom was home to protect me.

I imagine having my own Lifetime movie
Where for the first time ever, I will be in control of me
I want Keke Palmer to be me at 17 years old
And I want Angela Basset to be my mother
No father, no siblings.
No White people—
They ruin everything.
Just Angela and Keke.
Just my mom and me.

In this movie, Keke Palmer grows up to be a beautiful and happy
woman
There is no plot twist,
There is no sad ending,
And Keke is happy from beginning to end
And I am happy from beginning to end
And I am loved, the Black girl is loved
And the Black girl doesn't get abused,
The Black girl doesn't get abused,
The Black girl doesn't get abused.

JEZEBEL

It's nobody's fault but yours.
You should have worn longer pants,
Looser shirts.
You should have stayed away from the lip gloss and jewelry
Men will be men
Even if they are related to you.

You should have kept the smiles at a minimum
Should have told someone the first time it happened,
Because who is going to believe you after the third or fourth?
Your body betrayed you because you made her believe it was normal
By making him believe it was normal.

Hips and breasts and welcoming eyes,
He couldn't resist you
Beautiful.
Licentious.
Flamboyant.
Afraid.
You fit the description,
You fit the description well.

REASONS WHY I DON'T TALK MUCH

Nicole, we really have to get you to talk more. Cat got your tongue? Why don't you share what you feel?
The first time I stood up to him, he threw a book right at my face.
Walked around school the next day with a knot on my head, and told my friends that I fell off my bed
I can't sleep still, always rolling off that damn bed!
I couldn't tell them the truth.
Sometimes a cry for help can be a betrayal to silence
When silence is the only thing that is protecting you.
The second time I stood up to him, he used my mouth as his piss pot
Then strangled me when I spat it out all over his carpet that was already stained with my tears
I took the beating because I knew it was a matter of offering up my blood or my other half.
The fourth and final time I stood up to him, I was removed from my home by Social Services
While he remained comfortable and still in control
I got blamed for it, too.
When he told me that no one would ever believe me, he was right.
His mouth saved him while it crucified me.

To answer your question,
Cat never had my tongue,
Fear did.
Because every time I spoke up to protect myself, I dealt with the repercussions.

HOPEFULLY THIS WILL MAKE YOU UNDERSTAND WHY I DON'T DO RELATIONSHIPS

There was a guy in high school that I really liked
So, when he asked me to come to his house, I didn't hesitate
I didn't shave because that would have been my excuse just in case he had other plans in mind
There came a second and third opportunity
And after the fourth time, going to his house after school became part of my routine
I remembered the first time we kissed
And the second
And the third
And after the fourth time, he tried to take my clothes off
I told him that I wasn't ready because I was still recovering from my abuse
That's okay baby girl, I can make you feel good
Not sure if I was supposed to be pissed off because he said *that's okay* or called me *baby girl* or told me he could make me feel good
So, I decided to leave him be.

There was another guy I dated for about a year
Who made me believe that I was in love with him
I remembered when he told me he loved me.
There came a second and third *I love you,*
And after the fourth *I love you,* I was ready to give him my all
I told him that I wasn't ready because I was still recovering from my abuse
He said *damn, sorry that happened to you*
He also told me not to be too sensitive or vulnerable

Said *shit happens, can't let things hold you down forever.*
Not sure of how to respond, I decided to leave him be.

They both taught me a lesson—
Men will never understand what it's like to be a woman
And
They will not see anything wrong with abuse because their species
created it
And
They won't understand
They just won't understand
And
Not everyone deserves me or deserves to know the real me
Especially not anyone who chooses to normalize my pain.

AFFIRMATION

You are excellent
You are capable
Things will get better
Everything will work out for your good
Your story is not finished
You are still growing
You are loved
You are needed
You are irreplaceable

Don't give up on yourself.

FREE

I was a stranger in my own home
Chained down by fear of you attacking me,
I never left my corner.
Never made a sound because I did not want to awake any monsters,
And there goes silence saving me again.

You made sure of my discomfort every day.
I never knew who depression was until you introduced me to her
Until I caught myself questioning my own existence
It must be true when men say a woman has only one purpose
To GIVE
GIVE
GIVE,
And instead of being my protection,
You took advantage of my fragileness
You took from me what was supposed to be given to my first love
You took my voice, my emotions, my body,
While everyone remained unaware.

But I will no longer be a victim to these chains
You have wounded me, but you did not break me
As of today, I am learning to love myself for the first time ever
And I hope that my loved ones will be present to witness what survival
looks like
I pray that they will be patient with me
So that eventually, I could love them wholeheartedly
Because love heals all wounds,
But my wounds have not yet been healed.

WHO ARE YOU?

My name is Overcomer.
A normal life is what I have always painted in my pictures.
My favorite things to do are write, sing, and play tennis
I like to eat jelly and cheese on a whole wheat flatbread
I schedule crying appointments after having a rough day
I have a lot of self-doubt, and it is usually my loved ones who add fuel
to it
I like when life is predictable because I don't handle surprises too well
When I am in the passenger's seat, I like to be silent
There is something about the motion of a car that puts me at peace
with the world
Did I mention that I cry a lot?
Like a lot.
And please don't mistake that for weakness
I just haven't figured out a better way to handle sadness yet
I struggle with depression very often, and maybe after reading this
section you would understand why
As attractive as I am told I am, I'm not good with guys
I am not good with relationships or telling someone how I feel
I think about my future a lot.
Who will I marry? Will he be willing to understand me?
I think about heaven.
Will I already be healed before I get there?
Will I be able to meet people who have been through what I have been
through?
My name is Overcomer,
And I have survived.
I cheated death when I turned away from the hanger in my closet,
When I did not continue to walk at the red light
When I said no to the pills in my bathroom.

I am no longer afraid to be vulnerable,
Vulnerability can mend broken hearts.
I still have strained relationships with the people that I love
I try to be happy through other people's happiness
The best time for me to cry is between 11 p.m. and 1 a.m. when I am
not expecting any calls

Hell, I could cry all day because no one checks up on me anyways.

I have been through a lot if you haven't gotten that by now
And when I feel lonely, which is almost every night in my room
I tell myself this—
You are loved
You are not a mistake
You are not a failure
People look up to you
You are admired
Sleep tight, because joy will be right there when you wake up.

DEAR SELF

You are important. You are important. You are important.
You are important. You are important. You are important.
You are important. You are important. You are important.
You are important. You are important. You are important.
You are important. You are important. You are important.
You are important. You are important. You are important.
You are important. You are important. You are important.
You are important. You are important. You are important.
You are important. You are important. You are important.
You are important. You are important. You are important.
You are important. You are important. You are important.
You are important. You are important. You are important.
You are important. You are important. You are important.
You are important. You are important. You are important.
You are important. You are important. You are important.
You are important. You are important. You are important.
You are important. You are important. You are important.
You are important. You are important. You are important.
You arc important. You are important. You are important.
You are important. You are important. You are important.
You are important. You are important. You are important.
You are important. You are important. You are important.
You are important. You are important. You are important.
You are important. You are important. You are important.
You are important. You are important. You are important.
You are important. You are important. You are important.
You are important. You are important. You are important.
You are important. You are important. You are important.

You are important. You are important. You are important.
You are important. You are important. You are important.
You are important. You are important. You are important.
You are important. You are important. You are important.
You are important. You are important. You are important.
You are important. You are important. You are important.
You are important. You are important. You are important.
You are important. You are important. You are important.
You are important. You are important. You are important.
You are important. You are important. You are important.
You are important. You are important. You are important.
You are important. You are important. You are important.
You are important. You are important. You are important.
You are important. You are important. You are important.
You are important. You are important. You are important.
You are important. You are important. You are important.
You are important. You are important. You are important.
You are important. You are important. You are important.
You are important. You are important. You are important.
You are important. You are important. You are important.

11

Healing into Love

What happens when people open their hearts? They get better.
—Haruki Murakami

TO MY FUTURE LOVER,
I MUST SAY THIS

I apologize in advance for my brokenness
For trapping you into what you probably thought would have been
healthy from the start
I'm sorry that my body isn't new enough, and for all the abuse you
might taste every time you kiss me.
Maybe you won't even care
Maybe God is working on you just for me because he knows that I need
a special kind of love
Maybe you can help me heal,
I just don't want you to run away.
I'm sorry if I get offended every time you call me beautiful
I've never had a good relationship with that word because it often
portrayed that my life was beautiful too
I may have days when I cry unexpectedly, forgive me
I may fall into depression and ask for time alone, be patient with me
To my future lover I must say,
God is taking his sweet time with you
He is recreating you
Without spot or wrinkle
And I am excited to meet you
Excited to become familiar with your love
To finally fall in love.

I imagine how beautiful our children will be,
And when I give birth to them,
I will fall in love all over again.

God, I hope they aren't as sensitive as me

There I go beating myself down again
Forgive me, I do that a lot too.

I can't wait to be held by you, the man that I am supposed to love
And not who I am forced to love
So that I can look at you without fear and say *God, he was worth the wait!*
Dear future lover, I am dying to meet you
Dying to feel alive inside
Dear future lover, I hope that you are my first and last
I hope that you can look at me and smile
I hope that you will see past my flaw that has always been visible
Dear future lover, I see you in my dreams
And because of you, most mornings, I wake up happy
I wake up with love in my heart
Dear future lover, the thought of you is keeping me alive
It is keeping me sane.

Dear future lover, I am a jealous woman, forgive me.
I envy all the women who have come before me
Whose lips met with yours before mine could
But I will wait patiently because I know that God is working on you just for me
He is recreating you
Without spot or without wrinkle.

Dear future lover, I will read this to you on our wedding day
To prove to you that I have known you and have loved you all along.

TO THE BOY WHO SAID HE LOVED ME

You only say you love me
When we are laying side by side
Our lips are locked tight while my head is resting on your arm
We begin to set a mood in the atmosphere,
To become more intertwined,
To experience each other in a way we have never tried before
The only time you say you love me
Is when no one is around, just us
That is not love,
It's a lie.

INCAPABLE

You are more than your emotional labor.
If he doesn't express how grateful he is that you survived
So that he can show you what true love is
If he tells you that you are complaining too much
When you are only trying to help him understand you
Then he is not capable of giving you what you need
He is not capable of providing you with support
He is not worthy of you.

BROKEN WOMAN

Watchu cryin' for girl? Didn't the men in your family already tell you that your body was for giving?
I'm tired
I'm tired of having a mouthful of forgiveness
I'm tired of this body that has been clothed in silence
I'm tired of the breaking and entering
The mess
The screams that turned into daily routines
The unsolved mysteries
Of the girl's trespasser who was never found
Of the robbers who took a piece of me
Both the man and the woman.

I don't want to hear no sorry
Don't try to fix me neither
Just give it back, everything that you took from me
Including my peace of mind.

HIS PRESENCE, YOUR ABSENCE

He took advantage of me because he saw that you were never around
He then began to feel like he was the man in control of my life,
Because the man who was supposed to be the first to protect me,
To love me
Could not be found.

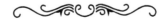

TRAUMA IN MY LOVE

I tell myself,
You are not deserving of happiness
How could I be worthy of something that has never made itself available
to me?
Never showed up to comfort me whenever my body was left in his
possession.
I found myself begging for pain to come around,
At least his showing up was consistent
His pep talks were *this will make you strong in any relationship you enter*
And now,
Whenever a man speaks, I hear his voice
Whenever I am given a demand, I see his face
When I attempted to lay with my first love, I felt his body pressed
against mine
Whenever a man grabs my arm, I hear that little girl pleading with him
to let her go.

Dear pain,
This did not make me strong in any relationship at all.
And the next time you visit, I need you to bring healing with you
Explain my situation to her and tell her that love still does not live here
Let her know that I am trying
Let her know that I want to love and I need to be taught
It is not easy when you have tried to love yourself just enough
To replace the love that everyone else failed to give you
Healing, I need you
I am trying to love,

I want to love,
I will be loved,
I will love,
Soon.

TO THE BOYS I DATED BEFORE 21

While sipping on my glass of red wine the day after my birthday, I
thought of you.
Don't flatter yourself, that was an inauthentic version of me
The version who lived for your approval
Who made sure that everything about her met your standards,
Cute enough, but not flashy
Educated, but not talkative
Sassy, but not so damn bitter
Black, but not too dark
Alive, but not living.
To the boys I dated before 21—
You will not take credit for the woman I have become
Your inability to help me grow does not count as giving me space to be
my own individual
You didn't care about any of that
As long as I stayed behind you, it didn't matter how fast I ran my race
To the boys I dated before 21—
I call 'em how I see 'em
Boys.
Immature, inconsiderate, incapable.
Unbelievable because for someone who had nothing to offer, you sure
expected a lot from me
You sure had a lot of rules regarding my life,
My body.

To the boys I dated before 21—
You were great practice before the real deal.

To the boys I dated before 21—
You have no idea what love is.

To the boys I dated before 21—
Remind me of a time you held any door open for me.

To the boys I dated before 21—
Why were you so insecure in your sexuality? In your masculinity?

To the boys I dated before 21—
I was sick and tired of being snuck into your parent's house.

To the boys I dated before 21—
You did not, do not know me.

To the boys I dated before 21—
Consider it a mistake.

SOMETHING I'VE HAD TO LEARN ON MY OWN

You have to believe that you're deserving of more
Or else you'll always accept the love that is thrown at you when you
are wanted
You deserve that *rub my back with coconut oil* love
That *let me massage your feet while you tell me how your day was* love
That *you relax for the evening, I'll cook dinner* love
That *I'll always show you how much you mean to me* love
If he doesn't express any of that to you, let him go for your sake
Holding on to him is only hindering you from finding the love that
God made only for you
I know it will be hard, but it's time that you put yourself first
You matter.

JUST RESIST

Resist modern-day slavery
Resist toxic relationships
Resist bad temptation
Resist unhappiness
Resist depression
Resist everything that does not bring you joy.

RESIST. RESIST. RESIST.

SOPHISTICATED MAN

Maybe one day
I'll build up the courage to tell you
That I am attracted to your happiness,
It keeps me alive
Thank you for seeing me as more than just broken glass,
More than just a project to be fixed
Thank you for pouring your joy into my heart.

READY

I am ready for love
I know this because every time I am with you,
I forget how horrible life has been to me
I forget my abuse,
The scars on my thigh
I forget how to hate
Because you show me
That I too can love.
You feel me
Every bit of my pain
From the fear in my eyes
To the trembling of my legs.
You held me
And for the first time ever,
Safety came to my rescue.

III

Blackness and Womanhood

The voice of a Black woman should always be herself. No edits, no erasure, no pressure, no expectations, no additions, no intruders.
—Malebo Sephodi

TO MY TWIN SISTER

My mom used to always dress me and my sister alike
Nicole and Nicolette, I put your clothes out already, y'all make sure the
shoes match
Make sure you put on the same jacket, and don't forget the matching scarves
and hats neither
Nicole and Nicolette this, Nicole and Nicolette that . . . I've never heard
our names called individually
If you got in trouble, I got in trouble too
And I hated it, and resented you.

Nicolette, the reason for this poem is because I never took the time to
express my deepest love for you
The reason for this poem is because I never told you how beautiful you
are and that the color of your skin is worth far more than gold despite
the invisible scars from lashes
No one will ever understand the pain that you and I share, we wear each
other's stories like straitjackets tightly clinging to the skin
We understand what trauma looks like, what it feels like
We know pain more than our mother knew awareness
More than our father knew presence.

My dear sister because we are Black and are women, this world has
already set out traps for us to fail
Stuck between a White woman's virtue and a Black man's vehemence
But Nicolette promise me that when they call you "angry," you will let
them know that they said "strength" incorrectly
And when they tell you that you're not pretty, you will assure them that
beauty shines both in and out of you

Negative people will live to place their own insecurities on you
What they say about you is only a reflection of themselves.

Black woman, let them understand that dark does not mean dirty,
Natural does not mean nappy,
And loud does not mean ghetto
You don't need no sunscreen
Your melanin is all the protection that you need,
Your melanin is resistance,
Your melanin is unconditional love.
The sun hides itself from you because you bring the heat,
Because you have a way of making people uncomfortable with your
miraculous presence
Nicolette, I adore everything about you from the thickness of your hair
to the thickness of your thighs
Never mind those blond streaks and blue eyes,
For your Blackness, no need to apologize
Remember, they want to be like you,
Ask Kylie.
Ask Rachel.

Sis, the reason for this poem is because even though I may not be five
or ten years older,
Those five minutes still count
So whatever you may ever go through,
Whether it be joy or pain,
You don't ever have to go through them alone.

TO BE A BLACK WOMAN

To the ten-year-old me,
If only you had a role model to look up to
To let you know that Barbie is not the standard of beauty,
YOU ARE BEAUTY
To be straight up with you
And tell you that some Black boys just won't like you if you're not light
enough,
Not White enough.
Now here I am
Trying to understand why a Black man who came from a Black womb
does not see worth in his own kind
Like Black isn't beautiful, like Black women aren't magical
Like we aren't the most educated group in America.

To be a Black woman is to be strong in the mind but weak in the body
Is to have our confidence mistaken for being ignorant and ghetto
Is to be seen as the cause of rape rather than the victim
My body was not made for your satisfaction, and my ancestors did not
endure all that pain just to see me go through them today

How am I supposed to find protection in a Black man who compliments
every woman but the ones who look like me?
Like his mother?
Like his sister?
To love a White woman more than your own is to be placed back in
chains
Is to disown the story of Emmett Till
Is to disown the stories of your ancestors
Is to prefer someone who robbed us of our features and called it
their own

The ones who want to be Black for the fashion, but does not want to acknowledge the trauma of being in a Black skin

And if this poem makes you uncomfortable,
Try dwelling in the world of a Black woman
Being asked to make several revisions to our appearance because the world will not accept us this way
Teaching our unborn sons to run from protection because they want them dead anyways
Constantly pleading to our daughters to protect their bodies,
Because a compliment can lead to rape.
Being ridiculed just for being Black and a woman and existing.

At least try to understand our story, and if this poem is *too Black* for you
Then please check your white privilege
Check your male privilege
Check your privilege.

DEAR BLACK GIRLS

Please continue to succeed and prove statistics wrong
I know it's hard to be an intelligent Black girl
When being academically successful is equated to "acting White"
But you know your full potential
Don't you ever quit

Dear Black girls
Make sure your parents buy you dollies that look like you
Because self-hate is the Devil himself
Your skin is filled with so much history and culture
Make sure you guard it with your life
Because with privilege, they can easily take it from you

Dear Black girls
For as long as I live, I will continue to love you unconditionally
Because you are truly precious souls
Souls that need to be protected from this world
This world that shows no interest in your well-being
In your existence
But dear Black girls, your existence is important to me.

DEAR BLACK GIRLS

I love you.
Please stay alive.
Please don't resist arrest.
Don't walk alone when the sun is down.
The enemy is usually out at night.
Please stay happy.
Please stay found.
Precious Black girls.

NO MORE ROOM

This world has been fighting against me from the time I left my mother's
I have been hypersexualized before I could understand what menstruation
meant
I have no room to slip up
To make men feel like it is okay to speak to me however they want
To touch me wherever they please
I am still fighting for natural rights
Still fighting for recognition,
For equality,
For the women who will come after me
I have no room to be weary
To rest for a few minutes,
Because this war is endless and it will not stop for a second
There are beautiful Black girls who look up to me
I teach them about the importance of self-love
I have no room to be sad
No room to show any signs of defeat
Even when I am weak, I must remain strong for their sake.
This world has given Black women no room for happiness or for peace
Yet we make room within our bodies to give life to the human race
We make room within our hearts to forgive those who have hurt us
This world was not created for a Black woman's living

We have been selfless for too long
It is time that we demand some damn space.

IMPORTANT RULES FOR THE WHITE GIRL

Don't touch my hair
Don't stare at my skin
Don't mock my culture and then steal it
Don't wear my cornrows and then rename it
Don't call me homegirl
I am not your homegirl
Don't tell me that your best friend is Black
Don't tell me you are not racist
Don't use my slang
Please, don't use my slang
And don't try to millie rock.

Signed, management.

LET IT FLOW, LET IT FLOW, LET IT FLOW

The first time I started my menstruation, I was sitting in my fifth-grade math class
My body felt different than any other day because pain was coming from an unfamiliar area
Nonetheless, I went with the flow,
Pun intended.
Fast-forwarding to lunch time, ignorant boy says to his friend *bro, do you see that red spot?*
Ignorant boy then calls me out and tells me to take my nasty ass home
And there I stood,
Frozen, hurt, and embarrassed.

The first time I started my menstruation was the first time I experienced being shamed
That was the first time I got a taste of what it's like to be a woman
Having to continuously fight the battle of being seen as a human being
To let men know that the blood I bleed every month does not give them the right to scorn me
It does not give them the right to call me dirty or crucify me as unclean

I have been taught that when I am on my period, I should always be silent and keep it to myself
I have been taught to embrace the pain and hide my pad in my back pocket when I need to go to the bathroom
Because letting the whole world know that I AM ON MY PERIOD is not lady-like.

To all period shamers who think that when a woman bleeds from her
vagina, she is now an untouchable—
The pain that we feel for several days is a testimony of our endurance
and strength
Your ignorance is making it hard for you to see that we hold all power
Ignore the magic if you want, but our vagina that bleeds the blood you
greatly despise has the power to start and end life
Thank us for your existence.

To the little girls who have not yet joined this journey—
Do not allow any little boy to make you a victim of shame
Your menstruation cycle does not make you less of a person
And if the pain is unbearable, scream your lungs out
If your period seeps through your pants, do not be discomfited
Those pants are replaceable, the value of your life isn't
The blood that you bleed is one of many attributes of your identity
You are the chosen one.
Embrace it, name it, love it,
PERIOD.

WHAT THE IGNORANT BLACK BOY IS BASICALLY SAYING IS

I hate Black girls
Those ratchet Black girls who act like they have no type of education
ingrained in them
I hate the way they speak, it ain't White enough.
And don't get me started on the way that they dress
But then they wanna complain about not being left alone like they
didn't draw the attention upon themselves
Black girls are not worthy of my attention
They are not worthy of any attention.
Why are they so ugly? And Black?
Why do they have bad attitudes? And are so damn angry all the time?
Why do they even exist?

I hate Black girls
And I refuse to love anyone who's unlovable
Untouchable.
I refuse to acknowledge Black girls
I refuse to compliment them too.
Until they learn how to be decent
How to be quiet and well educated,
How to stop using their history of pain as an excuse
And their mouths as a warzone,
Black girls will never be loved by me.

DEAR CATCALLERS

If you could just put your feet in a woman's shoe for a day,
Maybe you will understand how frustrating it is to experience street
harassment every time you step outside
Catcalling is not only annoying, it's also mentally damaging.

As a maturing woman, I have become conscious of the clothes I wear
Not because I think it looks tacky, but to prevent myself receiving
unwanted attention
To lessen the amount of whistling or *psst* that I will hear within hours.

Your catcalling also contributes to the degradation of women
We are not animals
We are not interested in hearing how fascinated you are with our bodies

Dear catcallers, I need you to understand that your harassment does
not boost my self-esteem
It makes me afraid to walk by myself even in broad daylight
It stops me from putting on my best outfits that I invested money in
When you catcall women, you are inferring that you do not value and
respect our existence
You are inferring that you only see us as walking sex objects.

Dear catcallers, if you still see nothing wrong with your approach to
getting a woman's attention
Then please catcall your mother and see how she responds to it.

IT'S BLACK WOMAN MAGIC

To the most marginalized group in AmeriKKKa—
I know it's hard having people see past your success but directly at your
struggles,
But you have proven history wrong so many times
You cannot be broken no matter how hard they try
Even when they cursed you, you prayed for them
When they took your children, you nourished theirs

You are the true definition of resilience
Anyone who stands before you look at you in awe,
Because everything about you is extraordinary
Damn Queen, you really are magical.

HERE'S HAIR

To the men who prefer straight hair—
No problem at all.
Just don't look at my curls and ask me why'd I leave the house like that
My hair is minding its business, you do the same.

To the men who started growing their hair to wear twist outs—
But our hair has been doing that for years
Where was our recognition?
Right, I get it
Patriarchy.

To the men who gets angry when they see my 'fro—
The next time you ask me what I am mixed with,
I will tell you Black and proud
And sorry for the disappointment
But my hair is here
It is here.
Like Miss Celie,
It is here.

DEAR BLACK WOMEN

One day they will bow at your feet and ask you to forgive them
One day the angry Black woman trope will be remembered no more
Ashe
One day happiness will be at your doorsteps
Somebody will tell them to stop dehumanizing you, I promise.
Someone will soon go to war for you
Ashe
It is time that you stop apologizing for being who you are
There is nothing to be apologetic for
One day they will realize that you are all-powerful
All-knowing
Ashe
You are heavenly
You are the closest to God
Dear Black women,
Your revolution will not be mistaken for man
It will not be reassigned while forcing you to stay silent
Ashe
Dear Black women, one day
Victory will be yours
Ashe
Victory is already yours.
Ashe

The poems in this section are not my own.
They have been written by five poets who have also chosen to be free.

These are their stories.

Name: A'nya Dunstan
Age: 8
Hometown: Brooklyn, NY

THIS IS ME

I am a butterfly,
I fly all day long.
When I fall, my wings will break,
But not my heart.
I will fly to the ends of the earth,
Until my wings can no longer flap
And my legs can no longer move
And the color of my wings turns gray.

I am a Black girl,
A Black girl with beautiful skin.
I admire my skin every day without a doubt.
I will not be ashamed of the skin that I am in.
I will love my skin.
Nobody can hurt or punish me because of my skin.
Other Black girls should be told how beautiful they are too.
And that their skin is their own symbol.

Butterflies and Black girls are similar because even though they may
both fall down, they still get back up again.

Name: Hunesher Dunstan
Age: 16
Hometown: Brooklyn, NY

HONEY AND GOLD

why is it that we only love our brown women when milk is rushing
down their backs
or
when they're rubbed up with oil?
but once that milk begins to spoil,
reaching hands begin to recoil
melanin that glisten gold compared to aluminum foil,
for it is forgotten that we are made of eternal sunshine and our
motherland's soil.
it's embedded within our coils,
our coils that surround
like a crown making our presence announced.
we're dipped in honey and gold
plump lips filled with stories untold,
let it be known that not an ounce can recreate our glory,
not saying that we're superior,
we are sacred—
better yet we're holy.

Name: D'Angelo Isaac
Age: 17
Hometown: Brooklyn. NY

UNTITLED

beautiful,
brown skin,
dipped in honey
with romance
lingering from an angel's hand

how beautiful can God make a person?

love in a liquid substance drippin'
from your veins
trying to catch every drop
so I can get drunk off it

If I ever had to paint a picture of my love
I would use my heart
as a paintbrush and paint

You are more beautiful than the
deepest
bluest
sea
because
see,
you are more beautiful than a sunflower blooming on top of a tree

that smile on your face tells a story

that I would read
over and over,
until I memorize every word,
and every sentence

that face,
I admire & appreciate,

and every cover girl has
no chance with you in any race
because you never cover girl in any makeup
all natural with a smile that makes angels want to steal it away
with a face that makes God praise

I am jealous of the mirror in your bathroom,
It gets more face time than I do,
it gets to look at your beautiful lips and eyes
even the days you are upset,
it sees your frowns,
even days when you're happy, it witnesses your beautiful smile.

Name: Demanie Redhead
Age: 14
Hometown: State College, PA

MY CULTIVATION

For years on end, I have let people walk all over me as if I were a sidewalk
Sometimes I feel that when I talk,
I am not heard.
I come to school feeling like I am drowning in a bowl of milk.
Everyone around me is White
I am done with feeling like I am not worth it,
Like I am not as pretty as the White girls around me,
Like am not smart enough.
I was always afraid of confrontation, thinking that if I spoke my mind
people would hate me.
Because how dare a Black girl open her mouth and speak?
But I have found my voice
And your only choice is to listen.
I have always told myself that I can't,
I can't be myself because people will not like me.
But should that even matter?
Why docs it take hiding behind a mask to fit in?
Or caking my face with makeup and wearing the tightest clothes just
to get noticed by a guy?
In society, we let beauty outshine intelligence,
But brilliance is the key
And I'm not afraid to go the distance it takes for me to succeed
I love who I am
I love that I am Black
You can try to sidetrack me, but my determination will always drive
me forward.

I regret ever wishing that I was popular, or that I could fit in and have a secure group of friends.
Because hiding behind a mask is not my task
My task is to let education help me gain power and make me do extraordinary things.
I will not settle for less
Because I am the best
And I am very blessed.
I am not a sidewalk
I am not a failure
I am not ugly
And I am not a follower.
I am a leader
I am Black
I am beautiful
I am strong
I am the definition of success
And whatever I conceive and believe, I achieve
I am guided and excited
What others think of me is not a concern
All I need in life is within me now
My confidence and competence are expanding every day.
I know that when I speak, my voice communicates strength, courage, and confidence
I am Demanie Redhead.
And I now set new and higher standards for myself
And I step up to every challenge in a state of absolute certainty and confidence
And for those who are not up to the challenge,
Have fun hiding behind your masks.

Name: Dana May
Age: 21
Hometown: Silver Spring, MD

DADDY

You have gone far too soon...
Leaving me with a crumbling world
which mockingly mimics the earth that rained over top your eternal bed.

And as I watched you be laid to rest,
I'm reminded of the words I allowed myself to bury and the pain I clung
to so that your feeble body would not have to.

But oh, how I wish you knew...
I wish you knew that your precious baby girl fell victim to devilish hands.
I wish you knew about how he boasted over his victory, plastering
"dreams really do come true" for the world to see.

I struggle to find my footing in this fatherless reality.
I desperately clutch onto habits that only seem to bear rotten fruit.
I have foolishly allowed their seeds to take root.
They have poisoned my mind and tainted my heart.
The person I am is no longer the person I was
and the uncertainty of my identity haunts me.

"Daddy, am I still your little girl?", I plead. He does not respond to me.
Instead, defeatedly I ask myself, "what would Daddy want me to do?"
"Who would Daddy want me to be?"
I chant and scream those words until they begin to pluck away at these
rancid roots.
And as the roots that once controlled me wither away.

Slowly, I change.

Flowers now bloom where desolate seeds took root. Butterflies replace
the moths that used to take poisonous flights within me.

The bottles I once drowned myself in, now collect dust.
The blunts my lungs once confided in have dwindle to ashes.
I have willing left behind all that no longer serves me.
"Daddy am I still your little girl? Please answer me"

"No baby girl, you have blossomed into a Queen.", He joyfully sings.

R.I.P Daddy 2/16/70 - 4/29/17

I did what my conscience told me to do, and you can't fail if you do that.
—Anita Hill

My conscience told me to share my story. To be free.

NOTES

"My life as a lifetime movie" was inspired by Ka'Lee Strawbridge who sat me down and read his poem to me when I was scared to share my own. Thank you.

"To the boy who said he loved me" well, you know who you are.

"Let it flow, let it flow, let it flow" was inspired by Dominique Christina. Thank you for being one of many women to erase the stigma on period.

"Here's hair" is dedicated to Black men who bash Black women for wearing their natural hair. Your opinions are discredited.

"Reasons why I don't talk much" is also reclaiming the significance of silence.

ACKNOWLEDGEMENTS

Thank you to the Xlibris publishing company for making this book possible for me. Thank you to my consultants, Maria and Jorge, for always being proficient and available.

Again, thank you to my aunt Charlyne for squeezing this book out of me.

Nicolette, thank you for surviving. Your presence gave me the courage to write these poems.

To my wonderful family both near and far, thank you for your continual support and love. To my sister Shaniqua, who is a best friend and mom all in one, thank you for your love and thank you for blessing me with Chase. To all of my little cousins who keep me going with their happiness and innocence, I love you.

To the Black community at Penn State, you are all amazing individuals. You inspire me each and every day I step foot into the Paul Robeson Cultural center. Keep striving and thriving. I am also thankful for all of my wonderful mentors at Penn State who helped me get to where I am today.

Thank you to amazing friends like Trisha Jolivert, Breeanna Bowen, Dana May, Whitney Brown, Theresa Dorsainvil, Brian Davis, Jade Knox, Beryl Bannerman, Sydni Jean, Mia Mighty, Dominique Smith, Darlyncia Nobrun and Danielle Clark for providing me with the space needed to be vulnerable and to simply be myself. Thank you to the college unions poetry slam invitational (CUPSI) team, Rabiyatu, Lara, Fatima, and Cleo for allowing me to be part of such a wonderful team of dope writers. Thank you to our coaches, Gabriel and Davon, and advisor, Mildred, for their honesty, tough love, and positive energy. Love you all. Thank you to Rachel McKibbens and Dominique Christina for coming to Penn State and sharing their poetry. You two are my inspiration.

To anyone who has been a victim of abuse, I understand. Free yourself of any guilt, self-blame, or self-hate. You are no longer a victim, you are an overcomer. The best is yet to come for you.

Lightning Source UK Ltd.
Milton Keynes UK
UKHW010254141120
373360UK00001B/67